MEGALOSAURUS

by Laura Alden
illustrated by Diana Magnuson

THE CHILD'S WORLD

MANKATO, MN

*Grateful appreciation is expressed to
Bret S. Beall, Research Consultant,
Field Museum of Natural History, Chicago,
Illinois, who reviewed this book to
insure its accuracy.*

Library of Congress Cataloging in Publication Data

Alden, Laura, 1955-
   Megalosaurus / by Laura Alden ; illustrated by Diana Magnuson.
      p. cm. — (Dinosaur books)
   Summary: Describes the physical characteristics, natural
environment, and habits of Megalosaurus, a huge, two-legged, meat
-eating dinosaur.
   ISBN 0-89565-629-9
   1. Megalosaurus—Juvenile literature.   [1. Megalosaurus.
2. Dinosaurs.]   I. Magnuson, Diana, ill.   II. Title.   III. Series:
Riehecky, Janet, 1953-   Dinosaur books.
QE862.S3A43   1990
567.9'7—dc20
                                                 90-42517
                                                    CIP
                                                    AC

MEGALOSAURUS

Many millions of years ago, the earth was a very different place. There weren't any people, but there were lots of dinosaurs!

After the dinosaurs died, some of their teeth, bones, and other parts became fossils. Scientists study these fossils and give the dinosaurs names. Usually the names tell how the dinosaurs looked or how they acted.

For example, the name Tyrannosaurus means "tyrant lizard," or, in other words, "Look out!"

Triceratops means "three-horned face"
—not a pretty sight, but a very good
description!

Pachycephalosaurus (PAK-EE-SEF-al-oh-sawr-us) means "thick-headed lizard." What a knock-out!

And Stegosaurus means "covered liz-ard," so named because of its cover of triangular plates.

If dinosaurs were alive today, they might not like their strange names. It may be just as well they're not around to com-plain.

The very first dinosaur to be named was the Megalosaurus (MEG-uh-low-SAWR-us). A museum in England had some mysterious fossil bones and teeth on display. At first, nobody knew what kind of creature the fossils belonged to. Then two scientists figured out that they belonged to a huge, extinct reptile. One of the scientists gave the creature the name Megalosaurus, meaning "big lizard."

Another huge, extinct reptile was discovered at about the same time. It was named Iguanodon, meaning "iguana tooth," because its teeth looked like the teeth of the iguana lizard. Scientists realized that Megalosaurus and Iguanodon belonged to a whole new group of animals. They named these animals, dinosaurs, the "terrible lizards."

For a while, some scientists called any big dinosaur they found Megalosaurus. It was quite a popular name. That would have surprised the Megalosaurus. It wasn't very popular while it was alive!

Soon, though, scientists realized that there were many different types of dinosaurs. They tried to figure out which bones really belonged to the Megalosaurus and which belonged to other dinosaurs. Then they tried to put the bones of the Megalosaurus together to see what it looked like. But they couldn't find enough bones to get a clear picture, and they made a lot of mistakes.

The Megalosaurus was really a huge, two-legged meat eater. But it took scientists a while to figure that out. One drawing of a Megalosaurus, done in the 1950's, showed it as a bear-like creature walking on four legs! Scientists hired an artist to make a model of this creature for the Crystal Palace in England.

Crystal Palace
London
England

Some scientists still confused the Megalosaurus with other dinosaurs. They showed it with tall back spines or a bony crest. In fact, there was only one thing the scientists always got right—its steak-knife teeth and razor-sharp claws. The Megalosaurus was *always* pictured as a mighty mean-looking dinosaur!

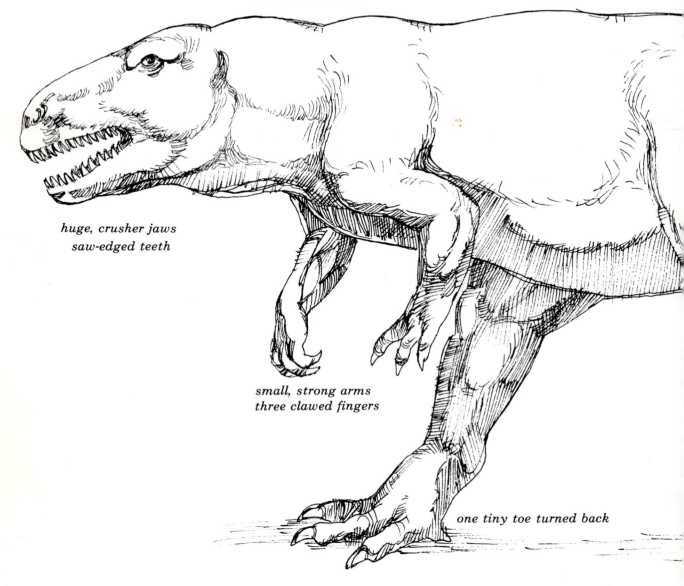

short, thick neck

huge, crusher jaws
saw-edged teeth

small, strong arms
three clawed fingers

one tiny toe turned back

Finally, though, scientists did learn what the Megalosaurus looked like. It stood about thirteen feet tall and could stretch out to almost thirty feet long. That meant it was nearly as big as a moving van!

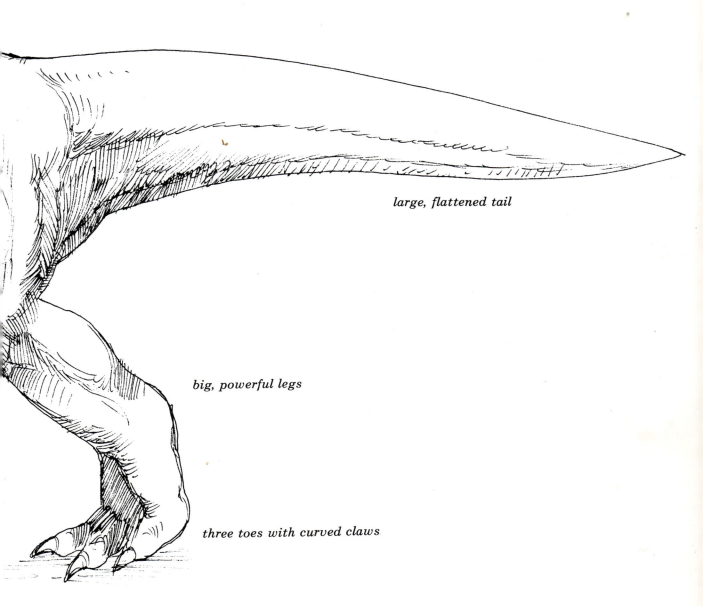

large, flattened tail

big, powerful legs

three toes with curved claws

The Megalosaurus weighed about a ton. That's very big—bigger than ten adults together—but it was much smaller than the terrible Tyrannosaurus, an even meaner meat eater that showed up later.

The Megalosaurus was mean enough, though. There were many huge plant eating dinosaurs that lived at the same time. The Megalosaurus undoubtably enjoyed them—for breakfast, lunch, or dinner!

The Megalosaurus could attack its prey with sharp, clawed hands and feet. It could tear at another dinosaur with its long, curved teeth. The Megalosaurus was definitely a ferocious dinosaur!

Though the Megalosaurus was fierce, it may also have been clumsy. Some scientists think its feet turned in slightly. If true, this would have made it hard for the Megalosaurus to walk. Only by keeping its tail straight out behind it could the

Megalosaurus be certain of keeping its balance. It might have even been funny watching the Megalosaurus stumble around. But back then, no one was laughing!

Plant eating dinosaurs didn't take time to laugh or cry when they saw a Megalosaurus. They ran! And on a bad day they might have had more than one Megalosaurus coming after them. Scientists have found footprints that suggest Megalosaurs traveled in small packs. That would have been really scary. One Megalosaurus hunting alone was bad enough. Facing a herd would have been much worse!

Scientists picture herds of Megalosaurs
roaming together on the plains or in the
buggy marshes, hunting for food. Other

dinosaurs may not have liked them, but
Megalosaurs liked each other.

As they hunted, Megalosaurs might have kept a look-out for a small dinosaur or two to feed their babies. Scientists don't know for sure, but some think Megalosaurs hatched from eggs and that the adults brought food back to a nest to feed their young.

Some also think that Megalosaurs protected their little ones. An adult Megalosaurus didn't have many enemies. (It was the enemy!) But a baby Megalosaurus was not as fierce. It could easily have been eaten by other dinosaurs. Still, with a Megalosaurus for a mother, the babies were usually safe.

No one knows exactly what happened to the Megalosaurus. It died out long before the end of the age of dinosaurs. Some scientists have suggested that a disease killed the Megalosaurus. Others think the temperature got too hot or too cold. Still others think that bigger, meaner meat eaters appeared and that the Megalosaurus just couldn't compete.

We may never know what really happened. All we know is that there are no more big and terrible lizards named Megalosaurus.

Dinosaur Fun

You can bring a dinosaur to life with your imagination! Imagine what it would be like to live with a Megalosaurus. Then write a story about it. You might begin your story this way: "I have a Megalosaurus for a pet." Describe what life is like with your king-sized pet. What kind of problems do you have? What is fun about being a Megalosaurus owner? Read through this book again for ideas.